Finding Your Purpose

By Spending 30 Days
in the Arms of GOD

by

Dr. Tracy Smiley-Thomas

Published by Watersprings Publishing, a division of Watersprings Media House, LLC.
P.O. Box 1284
Olive Branch, MS 38654
www.waterspringsmedia.com

Contact publisher for bulk orders and permission requests.

Copyright © 2020 by Dr. Tracy Smiley-Thomas

All rights reserved. No part of this publication may be reproduced, distributed, or transmitted in any form or by any means, including photocopying, recording, or other electronic or mechanical methods, without the prior written permission of the publisher, except in the case of brief quotations embodied in critical reviews and certain other noncommercial uses permitted by copyright law.

Scripture quotations marked "NKJV" are taken from the New King James Version. Copyright ©1982 by Thomas Nelson, Inc. Used by permission. All rights reserved.

Printed in the United States of America.

Library of Congress Control Number: 2020923567

ISBN-13: 978-1-948877-66-4

Table of Contents

	Introduction	1
DAY 1	You Are Praying But Are You Ready?	3
DAY 2	Performance or Purpose	9
DAY 3	Spread Your Wings So Others Can Fly	15
DAY 4	Stop Trying to Do God's Job	21
DAY 5	Seeking Perfection Without Reflection	27
DAY 6	Trust God Through the Process	33
DAY 7	God Has Permitted Your Test	39
DAY 8	Leaning On God vs. Leaning On Friends	45
DAY 9	You Will Never Conquer Worry	51
DAY 10	Your Purpose Is God's Funnel	57
DAY 11	Unbroken	63
DAY 12	The Hurt That Heals	69
DAY 13	Do Not Let Your Plans Interfere With God's Purpose For Your Life	75
DAY 14	God Knows Who You Are	81
DAY 15	Even in Your Struggles You Are Victorious	87
DAY 16	Pressing Forward in the Face of Adversity	93
DAY 17	Trace Your Time and Find Your Purpose	99

DAY 18	When Others Count You Out	105
DAY 19	God In Me is Enough	111
DAY 20	Learning to Fight God's Way	117
DAY 21	God Is Not Disturbed By Human Opposition	123
DAY 22	Being Effective vs. Being Seen	129
DAY 23	Mercy is Better Than Sacrifice	135
DAY 24	Traditionalist vs. Believer	141
DAY 25	Are You Missing Your Purpose?	147
DAY 26	Taking Time To Be in the Presence of God	153
DAY 27	Excellence in Worship	159
DAY 28	Tested and Purified By the Fire	165
DAY 29	You Are Not Defined By Your Season	171
DAY 30	Performance or Purpose	177
	Special Note From My Heart to Yours	183
	Special Thanks & Acknowledgements	184
	About the Author	185

Dedication

This devotional is dedicated in memory of my late mother Roxie Doll Smiley. I have never met a woman with so little, yet gave so much, I now understand the beauty that was inside of my mother. Everything that I am is wrapped up in God's grace and mercy along with what my mother taught me. Everything I have accomplished would not have been possible if my mother did not walk in the mercy, grace, and love of God. My mother unselfishly cared for my four siblings and I. A billion words could never describe my mother, but if I had to use one word it would be "resilient."

Mom you are gone, but no amount of time will ever make me forget your love, encouragement, and dedication.

Love, Your Baby Girl
TRACY

Introduction

We often miss God's plan and purpose for our lives. When our thoughts, deeds, or actions are not in alignment with God, our destiny or purpose will never be reached or fulfilled. Over the next 30 days as you seek to establish a closer walk with God, take some time to observe the miracles that already exist around you.

I share the words of this devotional with you to let you know that no matter what it looks like and no matter what you have been through, your situation does not have to be your destination. All you must do is give all your troubles, hurt, worries, disappointments, and defeats over to God and watch Him transform your life.

God is waiting to open the floodgates of your life. God has planted a seed in you that He desires to nurture. The God we serve is not boastful or forceful. God places many things inside of us and the ability to choose is one of them. Why not choose today to open your heart, mind, body, and soul to God. Allow God the time and room to manifest the destiny in your life that He has predestined. May your life never be the same after reading this devotional.

DAY 1

You Are Praying But Are You Ready?

Therefore take up the whole armor of God, that you may be able to withstand in the evil day, and having done all, to stand. Stand therefore, having girded your waist with truth, having put on the breastplate of righteousness, and having shod your feet with the preparation of the gospel of peace; above all, taking the shield of faith with which you will be able to quench all the fiery darts of the wicked one. And take the helmet of salvation, and the sword of the Spirit, which is the word of God.

EPHESIANS 6:13-17

Asking God for a favor or blessing is simple, for all you must do is ask. However, have you prepared yourself to receive the answer to the breakthrough that you have been asking about or praying for? As you pray every day trusting and believing in God, you must also be in a position to receive what God has for you. Prayer is an action word; therefore you must not only pray but move in the direction you desire God to take you. Is there something you can do while you wait on God? If God were to bless you today with whatever you have been asking for would you be ready not only to receive the blessing, answer, or breakthrough, but to hold on to it? Ask yourself, am I prepared for the blessing to come? If not, then what is it that I need to do to get prepared.

PRAYER

Dear God, I ask today not only for Your blessing,
but for Your direction as well.

Before you approach God in prayer
asking anything, pause and ask yourself,
am I prepared for the response that God will give?

Finding Your Purpose | 7

DAY 2

Performance or Purpose

Just as He chose us in Him before the foundation of
the world, that we should be holy and without blame
before Him in love, having predestined us to adoption
as sons by Jesus Christ to Himself, according to the good
pleasure of His will.

EPHESIANS 1:4-5

God has blessed each one of us with unique abilities and gifts, as well as the opportunity to utilize them. The question is, are you using the gift to be seen by men or for God to be seen through you? God has no issue with us being known, loved, or respected, but when our level of importance becomes more than His, we are seeking performance over purpose.

PRAYER

God help me to use Your blessing and gift for Your glory and not my own.

Finding Your Purpose | 11

You are created for God's purpose
and not men, for your uniqueness
fits your purpose.

DAY 3

Spread Your Wings So Others Can Fly

He gives power to the weak, and to those who have no might He increases strength. Even the youths shall faint and be weary, and the young men shall utterly fall, but those who wait on the LORD shall renew their strength; They shall mount up with wings, they shall run and not be weary, they shall walk and not faint.

ISAIAH 40:29-31

It is so easy to get caught up in ourselves and our own lives. It is easy to receive a blessing and get wrapped up in how great our lives are. However, true happiness and fulfillment come when we are not afraid to sow into someone else's life, goals, or dreams. God is happiest and most proud of us when others benefit from our blessing. Greater things happen and more can come to us when we spread our wings, so that others can fly.

PRAYER

LORD, please help me to be open to sharing what You have given to me with others. Help me to understand that my greatest success is not in my own success, but in the success of those You place in my path.

It is time to release all that has held you captive.

DAY 4

Stop Trying to Do God's Job

"For my thoughts are not your thoughts, nor are your ways My ways," says the LORD. "For as the heavens are higher than the earth, so are My ways higher than your ways, and My thoughts than your thoughts."

ISAIAH 55:8-9

God calls all of us to do our part in helping Him to reach others. However, God calls each of us for a specific purpose and that is to "go ye into the world and tell." God only asks us to share our miracles and blessings to let others know that He cares and that with God, there is no special person. God never asks you and me to convict or convert, only to tell others that God loves them and desires good for them. Stop telling and then dissecting. There is not one, only God has the ability and credibility to delve into the life of all those we come in touch with.

PRAYER

God help me to understand the part You have asked me to play, so that I do not cross boundaries that You have not designed for me to cross.

Finding Your Purpose

The more you move out of the way the more you will see God and the clearer your path will be.

Finding Your Purpose

DAY 5

Seeking Perfection Without Reflection

So Jesus said to him, "Why do you call Me good? No one is good but One, that is, God."

MARK 10:18

Therefore, you shall be perfect, just as your Father in heaven is perfect.

MATTHEW 5:48

Oftentimes we want everything to fall into place with little to no effort on our part. We want our lives to represent perfection, but we have spent very little time reflecting on why we are where we are. When we fail to reflect on the life that we have lived, we fail to open the avenues for the life that we have been destined for. Ask God today to give you the strength to face your past, so that you can walk into your future.

PRAYER

Father God, I ask today for wisdom to help me to reflect on where I am and have been, to better understand where You are taking me. The only perfection I will ever have is in You. Help me to reflect on the relationship I have with You.

Finding Your Purpose | 29

Seek inner spiritual peace by seeking the guidance of God through this journey called life.

DAY 6

Trust God Through The Process

Trust in the LORD with all your heart and lean not on your own understanding; In all your ways acknowledge Him, and He shall direct your paths.

PROVERBS 3:5-6

Continuously we say that we love and trust God, yet at the first sight of trouble or challenges, we question if God cares. Trusting God does not mean that our lives will be flawless, but it does mean our lives will be protected. Our faith and trust in God must go beyond the surface. Trusting God means digging deep. Hold tight and never let go of God's love, grace, and mercy. Trusting God means from the conception to the birth of an idea or situation, our trust, loyalty, and dedication are focused totally on God.

PRAYER

Father, I spend a great deal of time
trusting others, but today help me learn
the benefit and security that comes with trusting
You over and above anyone or anything.

Finding Your Purpose | 35

Lord, lead me and I will follow.

DAY 7

God Has Permitted Your Test

No temptation has overtaken you except such
as is common to man; but God is faithful.

1 CORINTHIANS 10:13A

Sometimes when we experience pain, heartache, difficulty, or disappointment the first thing we do is ask God "why". But do we ever stop to think that this test falls into the "all for my good" category? Nothing will ever happen in your life that God is not unaware. God must grant permission for any test or trial you may be going through. Whether it seems like it or not, in the end, it will be all for our good.

PRAYER

God help me to gain the courage and strength to understand and trust that all along You were in my life, and that all the things I have experienced will ultimately work out for my good.

God wants to take you to greater heights, but the journey will not be without trials or tribulations.

Finding Your Purpose

DAY 8

Leaning On God vs. Leaning On Friends

Trust in the LORD with all your heart, and lean not on your own understanding, in all your ways acknowledge Him, and He shall direct your paths.

PROVERBS 3:5-6

We say that we trust and believe in God; however, at the first sight of trouble, issues, headache, or pain, we tend to call on friends rather than God. Our first thought should be to reach out or call upon God, but we call or text a friend. What would happen if our first thought or instinct was to call upon God? Although friendships are necessary, the most important relationship is the relationship we have with God. We say we love and trust Him, but do we love Him enough to call upon Him first to give us direction and clarity rather than call on Him to clean up the mess that has resulted from the wrong advice.

PRAYER

Dear God, my desire is truly to serve You
and to put You first. Forgive me for doubting You.
Help me to lean on You rather than on friends
that may be here today and gone tomorrow.

At some point, even your friends will fail you,
but God will always be in your corner.

DAY 9

You Will Never Conquer Worry

Therefore, I say to you, do not worry about your life, what will you eat or what you will drink; nor about your body, what you will put on. Is not life more than food and the body more than clothing? Look at the birds of the air, for they neither sow nor reap nor gather into barns; yet your heavenly Father feeds them. Are you not of more value than they? Which of you by worrying can add on cubit to his stature? So why do you worry about clothing? Consider the lilies of the field, how they grow: they neither toil nor spin; and yet I say to you that even Solomon in all his glory was not arrayed like one of these.

MATTHEW 6:25-29

But seek first the kingdom of God and His righteousness, and all these things shall be added to you. Therefore, do not worry about tomorrow, for tomorrow will worry about its own things. Sufficient for the day is its own trouble.

MATTHEW 6:33-34

No matter how much time we spend pondering, walking the floor, missing sleep, or stressing, the thing called "worry" will never be conquered. God says, "Cast all your cares upon Me and I will give you rest" (1 Peter 5:7). The energy and thought that we place into worrying, trying to figure out what God has already worked out could be better spent letting others know that we are more than conquers.

PRAYER

Lord, teach me how to trust You.
You have promised to be my Guide.
I never will conquer worry, so why not
put my life, issues, and concerns into Your hands.

No matter how much time and effort you give to an issue or situation, you will never defeat worry, but with God, you are more than a conqueror.

Finding Your Purpose

DAY 10

Your Purpose is God's Funnel

Being confident of this very thing, that He who has begun a good work in you will complete it until the day of Jesus Christ.

PHILIPPIANS 1:6

We spend most of our lives focusing on our individual needs, wants, desires, dreams, and issues. We always try to figure out why did this happen to me or what is the lesson in this for each of us. Often our purpose for going through issues, heartache, and pain is because it is God's desire to use our lives as a funnel to reach others around us. We are the eyes and heart of God to those around us. No, we are not God, not even close, but if we are willing, we can become His vessels.

PRAYER

Father, give me clarity and understanding to know that for those around us, we are the vessel You pour from when seeking to reach others around us.

Finding Your Purpose

Allow God to melt, mold, and fill you.

Finding Your Purpose | 61

DAY 11

Unbroken

No weapon formed against you shall prosper, and every
tongue which rises against you in judgement You shall
condemn. This is the heritage of the servants of the LORD,
and their righteousness is from Me, says the LORD.

ISAIAH 54:17

Some have walked away. Some counted you out, and some have drug you through the mud. Someone reading this may have been abused mentally, physically, or emotionally. Someone reading this has been, rejected and disappointed, yet you remain unmoved and unbroken. Some of you were told that you will never amount to anything and no one else will ever truly love or want you. Someone reading this devotional has been bent, cracked, even shattered, but never broken. When you learn to trust God with your whole heart, no tragedy or disappointment will ever break your spirit because when you put your hands in Gods' hands you may hit the surface, but God will never allow you to hit the bottom. If your hands are in Gods' hands, you will remain unbroken.

PRAYER

Father God, help me to understand
that life and people may try to break me,
but when my life is wrapped in Your mercy
and then Your mercy says no,
help me to hold on to the fact
that I will never be broken.

Finding Your Purpose

Life can be unfair and difficult at times, but as long as you remain in the shadow of God nothing you experience will break you, because through the strength of God you are made strong.

Finding Your Purpose | 67

DAY 12

The Hurt That Heals

Is anyone among you suffering? Let him pray.
Is anyone cheerful? Let him sing psalms. Is anyone
among you sick? Let him call for the elders of the church,
and let them pray over him, anointing him with oil in the
name of the LORD. And the prayer of faith will save
the sick, and the Lord will raise him up. And if he has
committed sins, he will be forgiven.

JAMES 5:13-16

At no time in life do we ever feel good about pain no matter the cause. Oftentimes our greatest victory comes from our greatest pain. It is often in our pain that we find our purpose. We often do not see anything positive or helpful when we are hurting. Our minds do not go to the after, but the here and now. What would happen if we focused our thoughts on the other side of our pain? Think about the last big hurt. As it was taking place you were hurting and may have seen no way out, but when you came out on the other side you were better, stronger, and wiser, so the next time you are hurting just say to yourself this is only a test. It is always better on the back end, but you must exercise your faith and trust on the front end to be prepared for the reward on the back end.

PRAYER

Lord, help me to trust You even when it hurts.

The pain never feels good, but when
we come out on the other side of the pain,
our strength and resilience get stronger.

Finding Your Purpose

DAY 13

Do Not Let Your Plans Interfere with God's Purpose For Your Life

For I know the thoughts that I think toward you,
says the LORD, thoughts of peace and not of evil,
to give you a future and a hope.

JEREMIAH 29:11

Often, we make our plans without consulting God, so when God's ways and thoughts arise, we shutter them aside because they do not fit into our self-made plans. God has already told us that "our thoughts are not His thoughts and our ways are not like His" (Isaiah 55:8-9). It is not that God does not want to grant our wishes or desires, but if they do not align with God's will or desires, then they are a hindrance. Do not be so stubborn and self-centered that you miss out on all that God has for you. So, the next time you want to think on your own, just know that if your plans do not align with God's plans, they are simply a hindrance.

PRAYER

Father God, please forgive me for placing my own plans, wants, and desires higher than that which You desire for me.

Finding Your Purpose

It is God's desire that things in our
heart manifest; however, if your heart's desires
are not in alignment with God's purpose
for your life, do not expect God
to co-sign your plans.

Finding Your Purpose | 79

DAY 14

God Knows Who You Are

Before I formed you in the womb, I knew you;
Before you were born I sanctified you;
I ordained you a prophet to the nations.

JEREMIAH 1:5

There may have been times when others have pushed you away or aside. There may have been times when you have felt invisible, unwelcome, and unimportant. You may have sat in a room and felt like no one even knew that you were there. However, please know and understand that when all others have ignored or dismissed you that God knows who you are. It is time that you stop putting so much effort into trying to get others to notice you and more effort into getting to know who God is. The word of God says, "from the time you were in your mothers' womb, I knew you" (Jeremiah 1:5). Often, in the moments that you feel most alone is the time that God has allowed to bring you closer to Him. Remember the only recognition we really need is GOD.

PRAYER

Daddy, thank you for knowing who I am and assuring that the blood of Your precious Son Jesus Christ is the reason that I will never be forgotten.

You may appear to be invisible
or non-essential to others, but not to God.

Finding Your Purpose

DAY 15

Even in Your Struggles You Are Victorious

And he said, "Listen, all of you of Judah and you inhabitants of Jerusalem, and you, King Jehoshaphat! Thus says the LORD to you: 'Do not be afraid nor dismayed because of this great multitude, for the battle is not yours, but God's.'"

2 CHRONICLES 20:15

God's desire is that as you read this devotion you are not defined by what you have been through. The reason that you are victorious in your struggles is because the Victor lives within you. Struggles come not to break us, but to make us stronger. It is in your struggle that your faith is tested. Your struggle plus God equals Victory.

PRAYER

Father God, give me the strength to hold on and see You in my struggles, knowing that victory has already been promised.

See your life as a plane ride home to God, know that there may be some turbulence, rough winds, and layovers, but God will be standing at the home terminal of heaven with His arms open wide.

Finding Your Purpose | 91

DAY 16

Pressing Forward in the Face of Adversity

Have I not commanded you? Be strong and of good courage; do not be afraid, nor be dismayed, for the LORD your God is with you wherever you go.

JOSHUA 1:9

God wants you to understand that although you may be pressed on every side, do not quit. God's desire is that you press and push even when you do not feel like it. In the face of adversity understand that God will move things and people out of the way which seek to hinder you. Press forward in the face of adversity knowing that you are pressing your way toward God and all that He has for you.

PRAYER

Father God, provide me with the knowledge
and strength that I need as I press
in the face of adversity.

Finding Your Purpose

No matter what you are facing
stand tall and press forward.

Finding Your Purpose

DAY 17

Trace Your Time and Find Your Purpose

Plans are established by counsel;
By wise counsel wage war.

PROVERBS 20:18

When was the last time you sat down and analyzed how your time was spent? If each of us took time daily to trace our time we will find our purpose. We give our time, effort, and energy to that which we are interested in. God has designed and created each of us with a specific purpose in mind. If our time and energy are spent in an area that God has not designated or desired, then you and I cannot fulfill our purpose. Take some time today in the presence of God and ask Him to help you see where you spend your time so that you can find your purpose.

PRAYER

Father God, my true desire is to honor
and fulfill the purpose that You
have designed for me.

Finding Your Purpose | 101

There is nothing wrong with following your dreams, as long as you remember the dream giver.

Finding Your Purpose

DAY 18

When Others Count You Out

When my father and my mother forsake me,
Then the LORD will take care of me.

PSALM 27:10

Each of us has experienced loss, hurt, and rejection at some point in our lives. Due to choices or circumstances, we sometimes find ourselves in positions that are not welcomed or desired. I am a firm believer that no one wakes up with the intention of being in an undesirable place or space. When things do not work out as we thought they would, we still must find a way to push on. However, often there are some individuals in our lives who count us out and walk out because we are struggling to get it right. When friends and family walk away or wipe their hands of us, God has promised to "never leave us nor forsake us." (Hebrews 13:5) Just know that "God is a friend that sticks closer than a brother." (Proverbs 18:24)

PRAYER

Father God, thank You for not leaving me in my mess. Thank You for wrapping Your arms around me and never letting go.

Finding Your Purpose

Allow God to release you from your past.

Finding Your Purpose

DAY 19

God in Me is Enough

For God so loved the world that He gave His only
begotten Son, that whoever believes in Him should not
perish but have everlasting life. For God did not send
His son into the world to condemn the world,
but that the world through Him might be saved.

JOHN 3:16-17

Oftentimes we desire, seek, and look for things, people, jobs, and possessions thinking that any of those things will complete us, or make us happy. Only to find out that at the end of it all, we are still lonely and empty. God's desire is for us to understand that above and in everything that He is enough. God's desire is for us to be fulfilled and happy. However, it hurts Him to know that we seek other things to fulfill us or make us happy. God wants us to know that when He allowed His Son to stretch out His arms for you and me, that meant He alone is enough.

PRAYER

Father God, please forgive me for thinking that I could ever find someone or something else to do what only You can do. And helping me to see that with all that You have done in my life, that You in fact are enough.

Finding Your Purpose

Make God the driving force of your life.

Finding Your Purpose | 115

DAY 20

Learning to Fight God's Way

Pray without ceasing.

1 THESSALONIANS 5:17

When we are faced with difficulty, hurt, or pain, rather than look to God for the answer or direction, we often set out on our own to fix the problem, pay someone back, or to get even only to find that we are no better off than where we started. God says, "Lean not to your own understanding, but in all your ways acknowledge him and he shall direct your path." (Proverbs 3:5-6) God is patient and kind. God is a thinker and a planner. God never acts or reacts, but in His own time and ways, knows the how and the when and fights in a fair manner. What would happen if we tried things God's way rather than our own? We take time to learn everything else, but how much time do we spend learning to fight God's way? We can only know His ways by spending time with Him.

PRAYER

God please send the Holy Spirit to show me how to fight Your way, and not my own.

Finding Your Purpose | 119

The first instinct of human beings
is to get even or to seek revenge,
but God has promised to fight your battle.

Finding Your Purpose | 121

DAY 21

God is Not Disturbed by Human Opposition

For we do not wrestle against flesh and blood, but against principalities, against powers, against the rulers of the darkness of this age, against spiritual hosts of wickedness in the heavenly places.

EPHESIANS 6:12

God is so patient and kind that He allows each of us to make our own choices and decisions. However, He is neither bothered nor disturbed by our opposition. God is the Alpha and Omega the beginning and the end, all-knowing and consistent. When God has a plan for our lives, no matter how much we fight, resist, or ignore Him it shall happen. God says, "His ways are not like ours, nor His thoughts like our thoughts" so what makes us think that we can outsmart God. No matter the difference or roadblock, God can and will finish that which He has started.

PRAYER

Father God, forgive me for getting in Your way, and often serving as my own stumbling block.

Finding Your Purpose

God allows each of us to make
free, independent choices.

DAY 22

Being Effective vs. Being Seen

But the LORD said to Samuel, "Do not look
at his appearance or at his physical stature,
because I have refused him. For the LORD does not
see as man sees; for man looks at the outward
appearance, but the LORD looks at the heart."

1 SAMUEL 16:7

Is it your desire to add value and purpose to a life other than your own? Do you desire to spread your wings so that others can fly? God grants each one of us the ability to exercise our individual gifts, but the issue at hand is are we using our gifts to be effective, or to be seen? There is nothing wrong with shining, but if our shine does not evolve into effectiveness for others around us, then the gift is useless and without purpose.

PRAYER

Father God, help me to use my skills and abilities to help make someone else's life better. Help me to be effective rather than just being seen.

Finding Your Purpose

Being and existing is one thing; however, being effective is another.

Finding Your Purpose

DAY 23

Mercy is Better Than Sacrifice

For judgement is without mercy to the one who has shown no mercy. Mercy triumphs over judgement.

JAMES 2:13

Daily we encounter individuals who face issues and challenges which we are aware of and may offend us in some way. God desires mercy over sacrifice. When we esteem others better than ourselves, the love, grace, and mercy of God will always cover, guide, and protect us. Love always wins. Love is an extension of mercy. The next time someone hurts, disappoints, or offends you, remember mercy is always better than sacrifice.

PRAYER

God, moment by moment Your mercy I see.
Help me to show others the same
grace and mercy You show me daily.

Finding Your Purpose | 137

To sacrifice is one thing,
but to experience the mercy of God is another.

Finding Your Purpose

DAY 24

Traditionalist vs. Believer

So they said, "Believe on the Lord Jesus Christ, and you will be saved, you and your household."

ACTS 16:31

We wake up every morning hopefully spending some time with God, but how often do we self-examine to determine if we are a traditionalist or a believer. Do we talk to, believe in, and serve God because we believe, or is it because we have been taught to do so? Do we trust God with our heart, mind, body, and soul because we were taught from a child to do so? We must daily examine our lives and ask ourselves do I honor God because I believe or because it is the right thing to do? Traditionalist or Believer, which are you?

PRAYER

God, I love and honor You.
My relationship with You is because
I believe that You are who
You say You are, and will do
what You say You will do.

Finding Your Purpose | 143

It is one thing to know
and another to believe.

Finding Your Purpose

DAY 25

Are You Missing Your Purpose?

There are many plans in a man's heart,
nevertheless the LORD's counsel-that will stand.

PROVERBS 19:21

From the moment you were in your mother's womb, God knew you (Jeremiah 1:5). God knows the number of hairs on your head (Luke 12:7). Your steps are ordered by God (Psalm 37:23-24). Each of us has a life that has already been predestined by God. It is God's desire that we live full, productive lives. We are all given free will to choose each day what we say and do; however, it is possible that because we often choose a path different than God desires, we miss our purpose. Each of us has been given or trusted with a specific purpose that only we can accomplish. Ask yourself today if the life that you are living is taking you closer to, or further from where God wants to take you? Are your choices or decisions helping you to accomplish or achieve your purpose or causing you to miss out on your purpose?

PRAYER

Father God, help me to know when You are talking to me. Give me the strength and courage to focus on You so that I do not miss my purpose.

Finding Your Purpose | 149

You may be busy, but are you fulfilling your God-given purpose?

DAY 26

Taking Time to Be in the Presence of God

You will show me the path of life; In Your presence
is the fullness of joy; At Your right hand
are pleasures forevermore.

PSALM 16:11

From the moment we open our eyes, we plot and plan our day. We make time for our loved ones, friends, job, hobbies, goals, and our dreams, but how much time do we spend with ourselves thinking about God? We must view God as more than a funnel for our needs or wants we would begin to see that He is so much more. God desires our lives to be full of promise and purpose, but do we see Him as a stumbling block rather than the One who desires the best for our lives? When we learn to take the time to sit and talk and hear God, we will find all the answers to our problems. Freedom from self-afflicted bondage and the need to please others is not the answer. It is time to see God as the air we breathe and the beat of our hearts. It is important that we spend quiet uninterrupted time with God. Take the first step today by spending time with and being in the presence of God.

PRAYER

God forgive me for putting everything ahead of You. Today, I purpose to take time to be in Your presence.

Finding Your Purpose | 155

When you stop and listen,
it is then that you will see and hear God.

Finding Your Purpose

DAY 27

Excellence in Worship

And Jesus answered and said to him, "Get behind Me, Satan! For it is written, 'You shall worship the LORD your God, and Him only you shall serve.' "

LUKE 4:8

We spend time daily striving for excellence in our jobs, in school, or completing selected tasks. However, we spend very little time focusing on excellence in worship. If we can give our all in everything else, why do we neglect to give our all to God? Excellence in worship means giving God our first and best. Excellence in worship means being connected to God in every aspect of life. Excellence in worship means that God is enough, my refuge, and guide. Excellence in worship means treating others better than I want to be treated. Excellence in worship means totally trusting God when things get cloudy. Excellence in worship means total surrender and trust in God. Excellence in worship means LORD You lead, and I will follow.

PRAYER

Father, on my own I can never achieve excellence, but in Your presence, I am excellent because the blood of Jesus paid it all. When I said yes to You all was made new. Now teach me to walk in Your excellence.

You put forth your best in everything else, but how would you rate your worship?

Finding Your Purpose

DAY 28

Tested and Purified by the Fire

> That the genuineness of your faith, being much more precious than gold that perishes, though it is tested by fire, may be found to praise, honor, and glory at the revelation of Jesus Christ.
>
> 1 PETER 1:7

In life, we all at some point will face trials and disappointments. God has told us in His word that "No weapon formed against us shall prosper." (Isaiah 54:17) God did not say it will not form, but He did say it will not prosper. When was the last time you faced difficulty or heartache? While enduring tests and trials the hurt we feel becomes almost unbearable. However, when we come out on the other side, we are stronger and better. God allows trials to prepare us for what lies ahead. Stop looking at the trials or tests you face as a stumbling block, rather see them as road maps to your destiny. As long as we live, we will be tested and purified by the fire.

PRAYER

God, you promised to never leave me nor forsake me. (Hebrews 13:5) Help me to know and understand that the test is but a ticket; thus, fire will only purify what You have already purified.

Finding Your Purpose

You have been bruised, battered, and bent, but never broken.

Finding Your Purpose

DAY 29

You Are Not Defined By Your Season

To everything there is a season, a time for every purpose under heaven: A time to be born, and a time to die; a time to plant, and a time to pluck what is planted; a time to kill, and a time to heal; a time to break down, and a time to build up; a time to weep, and a time to laugh; a time to mourn, and a time to dance; a time to cast away stones, and a time to gather stones; a time to embrace, and a time to refrain from embracing; a time to gain, and a time to lose; a time to keep, and a time to throw away; a time to tear, and a time to sew; a time to keep silence, and a time to speak; a time to love, and a time to hate; a time of war, and a time of peace.

ECCLESIASTES 3:1-8

Our lives are predestined by God, but that does not mean that we will not go through some things. Your past mistakes are just that "mistakes". But God wants you to know and understand that your situation does not have to be your destination. You are not defined by the season of life that you are currently in. There are four seasons in a year, but just as each season comes, it must also go; and so shall your mistakes and disappointments. The next time someone tries to remind or define you by what you used to be, just simply remind them that God has already cast your sins and mistakes into the sea of forgetfulness, so you suggest they do the same. The next time someone wants to dredge up your past simply remind them that you are not defined by your season.

PRAYER

Father God, thank You for not only forgiving me, but also for reminding me that I am not defined by my season.

Finding Your Purpose

Your situation does not have
to be your destination.

DAY 30

For Man Or For God

For we are His workmanship, created in Christ Jesus
for good works, which God prepared beforehand
that we should walk in them.

EPHESIANS 2:10

With the gifts and talents that you have received, do you use them to perform and be seen or do you use them for the purpose of trusting and honoring God? If we are honest with ourselves each of us likes to be seen, heard, liked, and applauded, and while none of these things in and of themselves are bad, pride can quickly change things. God does not see us when we are simply performing, but He does see us when we live our purpose. Are you working for the applause of men or for the reward of God?

PRAYER

God, my true desire is to live with purpose.
Help me to care more about You
and how You see me, and less about
the temporary applause.

Finding Your Purpose

No matter what you are dealing with today,
a better tomorrow is coming.

Special Note From My Heart to Yours

Every woman that reads this devotional has made a choice to spend more time with God. It is my sincere hope that the next 30 days will be life-changing for each of you. The titles selected for each day come directly from my heart. Personally, I have had to address each of these areas in my life. My ability to survive and write this devotion symbolizes the capability of God. After you have completed your own reading, please share your devotion with someone else. As I seek wholeness and wellness, I desire the same for each of you. Although we may not have met, my heart has already connected to yours. It is through my personal journey that I can share the words within this devotional with you. May the grace of God rest, rule, and abide with each of you.

DR. TRACY SMILEY- THOMAS

Special Thanks & Acknowledgements

I spoke earlier about some of the incredible women that God has placed into my life. Deborah Patterson is one of those women. Not only have I sat and shared with her, but she is responsible for assisting me in matching each devotion topic with a scripture so that you can not only be inspired daily, but also become more connected with God's Word and see how it applies, not only to our eternal salvation, but to our everyday lives.

About the Author

My name is Tracy Smiley-Thomas. If I can be transparent, the pain, hurt, and rejection that I have felt over my life fueled this devotional. I come from very humble beginnings, raised along with my four siblings, by a single mother. What my mother lacked in material goods she exceeded in love and structure. One of the hardest things I have ever had to conquer was growing up never knowing what my father looked or sounded like. By the age of 19, I was a single mother of two boys and a high school dropout. To support myself and my sons I earned my Certified Nursing Assistant Certificate (CNA).

After working as a (CNA) for several years I made the decision to enter the US Army, but to do so I would need to earn my General Education Diploma (GED) and 24 semester hours of college credit. With hard work and the promises of God, I achieved my goal. In September of 1994, I was sworn into the US Army in Montgomery, Alabama. In 2002 I became a Licensed Vocational Nurse, and in 2012 I became a Registered Nurse. While enrolled in dual nursing programs, Bachelor of Science in Nursing (BSN) and Master of Science (MSN) with a Specialization in Nursing Education. I have had the privilege for nearly five years to serve as nursing faculty for an Associate Degree Program in Georgia.

While writing this devotional and navigating through COVID-19, I am proud to say that I earned the degree of Doctor of Philosophy with a specialization in Nursing Education (Ph.D.). God has placed some phenomenal women in my life that have helped me through some very difficult times. If I could leave one thing with you it would be that God will do what He has promised. I look forward to becoming a part of your daily connection with God.

CPSIA information can be obtained
at www.ICGtesting.com
Printed in the USA
JSHW040956060322
23451JS00002B/9

9 781948 877664